The
Cast Iron Cookbook
Amazing Cast Iron Skillet
Breakfast Recipes this summer

By

Elizabeth Scott

Table of Contents

Health Reasons to Cook with Cast Iron Skillet

Cast Iron skillet is a Chemical-Free Alternative to Nonstick Pans

Another bonus to using cast-iron cookware instead of nonstick pans is, you avoid the dangerous chemicals that are seen in nonstick pans. Repellent coatings found in nonstick pans contain PFCs (perfluorocarbons), which keeps food from sticking to the nonstick pots and pans and it's linked to liver cancer, liver damage and, according to a study in the *Journal of Clinical Endocrinology & Metabolism*. Perfluorocarbons (PFCs) get released and inhaled from nonstick pans form of fumes when they are heated on high heat. Also, we can ingest these PFCs when surface of pan is scratched. Both ceramic-coated and regular cast-iron pans are perfect alternatives to nonstick pans for this health reason.

Cooking with Cast Iron Fortifies Your Food with Iron

Being certain that cast iron does not leak chemicals, it can as well release some iron into your food, which is a good thing. Iron deficiency is quite common globally, particularly among women. About 10% of women living in the U.S are iron-deficient. Cooking something acidic such as tomato sauce within a cast-iron can increase iron content, twenty times more.

You Can Cook With Less Oil When Using a Cast-Iron Skillet

That beautiful sheen on the cast-iron skillet renders it virtually nonstick, the sign of a well-seasoned pan. The health benefit, of course, is you would not need to use gads of oil to sear chicken when cooking in cast-iron or brown crispy potatoes .In order to season your cast-iron cookware, cover the bottom of the skillet with a strong layer of kosher salt and ½ inch of cooking oil. Then heat till oil begins to smoke. Pour the salt and oil carefully, into a bowl. Then use 1 ball of paper towels to rub the inner part of the pan till its smooth. In cleaning your cast iron skillet, never use soap. Just scrub it with stiff brush, adding hot water and then dry the skillet completely.

How To Get The Best Out of Your Cast Iron Skillet

Let it get dirty

Whatever you do, do not use washing up liquid on your skillet! The soap will soak into the iron fibers of the pan and coat all of your food in an unwanted soapy seasoning. Instead, simply rinse the skillet with warm water, allowing it to soak then gently scraping large pieces of food from the bottom.

Make it non stick

In order to make your skillet as effective as those exorbitantly expensive non stick pans, simply cover it in a thin layer of canola oil and bake in a hot over for 90 minute. And voila! Pancakes will be sliding over your skillet like butter.

Be creative

You'll be amazed how many dishes you can cook in the skillet, and how resilient they are, so don't be scared to try new and daring recipes. Their enduring quality means they're fine to place in the over, allowing you to rustle up cakes and frittatas with minimal washing up.

Cast Iron Catalan Sauté of Chicken with Sausage, Capers & Herbs

Ingredients

- 3/4 teaspoon kosher salt, divided
- 1 1/2 pounds whole chicken legs, thigh and drumstick separated
- 2 teaspoons peanut or canola oil, divided
- 8 ounces sweet Italian turkey sausage links
- 1/4 teaspoon freshly ground pepper, plus more to taste
- 2 large tomatoes, diced
- 2 teaspoons butter
- 1 large shallot, minced
- 1/2 cup white wine
- 2 large cloves garlic, crushed and peeled
- 1 sprig fresh thyme
- 1 1/2 teaspoons cornstarch
- 1 sprig fresh rosemary
- 1/2 cup reduced-sodium chicken broth
- 1 teaspoon freshly grated lemon zest
- 2 tablespoons capers, rinsed
- 2 tablespoons finely chopped flat-leaf parsley, for garnish

Method

- Remove chicken skin, trimming off excess fat and season chicken with 1/4 teaspoon pepper and 1/2 teaspoon salt.

- Heat one teaspoon of canola (or peanut, as preferred) oil in your skillet, over medium heat. Toss in sausage and sauté, turning often, till browned on every side, about seven minutes. Then transfer onto cutting board; leave to slightly cool, slicing crosswise to half-inch thick rounds.

- Toss in the remaining one teaspoon oil with butter onto your skillet, increasing heat to a medium high. Add chicken and cook. Turn often till browned on each side, about four to five minutes and transfer onto a plate.

- Add garlic, tomatoes, shallot, pepper and the remaining 1/4 teaspoon salt to the skillet and cook. Stir often till most of its liquid has been evaporated, about seven to nine minutes. Add rosemary, thyme and wine and continue to cook, stirring often, about two to three minutes. Then return the sausage and chicken to the skillet and keep turning so as to coat them with sauce. Then cover and leave to simmer till sausage and chicken are well cooked, for fifteen to twenty minutes

- Mix cornstarch and broth together till smooth, in small bowl. Ladle the sausage and chicken into serving dish, using slotted spoon. Pour away the thyme sprigs and rosemary. Set lemon zest, capers and cornstarch mixture into the skillet. simmer and cook till skillet juices become thickened, about one to two minutes. Serve chicken with the sauce. If desired, garnish with parsley.

Cast Iron Cinnamon Apple Crisp

Ingredients

- 1/2 cup rolled oats
- 1/2 cup brown sugar
- Pinch of salt
- 1 tablespoon butter
- 1/4 cup of white sugar
- 1 teaspoon cinnamon
- 3 – 5 baking apples

Method

- Preheat your oven to 350-degrees and grease a cast iron skillet lightly, with butter.
- Peel apple core and slice to bite-sized pcs. Mix cinnamon, white sugar and apples together, pouring mixture to your cast iron skillet.
  Combine the rolled oats, brown sugar, salt and butter together in a bowl, using back of a fork .Ladle mixture over apples.

- Then bake for thirty to thirty-five minutes till apples become bubbly and stender, with topping being golden and crisp.
  As desired, serve with whipped or ice cream.

Cast Iron Sunday Steak with French Butter

Ingredients

- 1stick unsalted butter

- 1 1/2tablespoons flat leaf parsley, chopped

- 2porterhouse steaks, 1 pound each

- Kosher salt

- 1teaspoon shallot, minced

- 1/2teaspoon garlic, minced

- Half a fresh lemon

- Oil

- Freshly ground white pepper

Method

- Place the steaks on a cooling rack which is set over tray with edges, at least six hours before cooking them. You don't want to lose the drips
- Use salt to season every side of the steak and put them back into your refrigerator, leaving it uncovered up to 1 hr before cooking.
- Using pestle, pulverize and crush the shallot, parsley and garlic in a mortar till they become mushy.
- Allow butter to soften at room temperature and ladle it in a small mixing bowl. With the butter, add a few drops of lemon juice, the

aromatics, a few grinds of white pepper, a pinch of salt. Blend butter till it becomes a shade of green without any streak.

- Roll the butter up in parchment pepper or refrigerate as is. Foil, twist each end to form round log. Foil leaves ends to remain sealed.
- Whenever you are set to prepare the steaks, use fresh ground black pepper to season both sides. Set a skillet over fairly high heat and pour enough oil to ensure the skillet is well coated. add the steak when oil becomes hot(not too hot) and Cook them on both sides till it's caramelized and browned. Remove steak from skillet and set on a sheet tray.
- Cook the other steak likewise .you can cook the steaks close to 1 hour and leave to cool at room temperature and should not be refrigerated.
- Place the top rack, about eight to ten inches in your oven and heat the broiler.
- Chop the meat off the bones and cut into small sizes, using a filet knife. Re-arranging the steaks on sheet tray, coat them steak with butter and set a little glob on every steak.
- Transfer steaks below the broiler just enough to melt the butter. Heat the steaks thoroughly and serve

Cast Iron Veggie Confetti Frittata

Ingredients

- 1 tablespoon butter
- 3 (8-oz.) baking potatoes, peeled and shredded (about 3 cups firmly packed)
- 1 small red bell pepper, diced
- 2 tablespoons vegetable oil
- 1 garlic clove, pressed
- 1 medium onion, diced
- 6 eggs
- 3/4 teaspoon salt, divided
- 1/4 teaspoon pepper

Method

- Heat your oven to about 350°c and set the sliced potatoes in a bowl. Cover with cold water and leave for about five minutes. Then drain and dry.
- Heat a knob of butter with oil in a skillet over medium flame. Add onion and bell pepper and sauté for about three to minutes or till soft. Add garlic and cook for one minute. Pour in the sliced potatoes with 1/2 teaspoon salt. Stirring often, cook for ten minutes or till potatoes become tender and golden.
- Remove the now, tender potatoes from heat. With the aid of a spoon, make six impressions in potato mixture. Then Break an egg each into the impression. Sprinkle pepper and the remaining 1/4 teaspoon salt on the eggs.
- Place in oven and bake at 350° for twelve minutes or till eggs become set and serve immediately for a delicious breakfast.

Cast Iron Sausage Gravy and Biscuit Skillet

Ingredients

- 4 Tbsp unsalted butter
- 1 lb sage breakfast sausage (bulk
- 3 cups milk
- 4 Tbsp all-purpose flour
- 2 tsp fresh ground black pepper
- Optional garnish: fresh parsley, chopped Drop Biscuits
- ½ cup shredded Parmesan cheese
- 2 cups all-purpose flour
- 1 Tbsp granulated sugar
- 1 Tbsp baking powder
- ½ tsp kosher salt 1 cup whole milk
- 1 Tbsp granulated sugar

Method

- Heat oven to about 450°F. Cook sausage till lightly browned, in a skillet over medium high heat. Remove sausage from skillet and place in a bowl, using a slotted spoon.
- Meanwhile; combine baking powder, flour cheese, salt and sugar, mixing with a fork till well combined. Stir in milk with a fork till mixture blends together and set it aside. Melt butter in a hot skillet, sprinkling flour over butter. Then whisk together.
- Leave mixture to bubble for about two minutes to sauté out its floury taste, whisking often. Whisk in milk to combine and endeavour to pick up little bits of sausage on the base of skillet (makes great flavor). Leave gravy to bubble for three minutes and the mixture will begin to thicken. Add sausage and black pepper back into the skillet, stirring to combine.

- Remove mixture from heat and set skillet on cookie sheet. Add¼ cup scoop biscuits to pan. Spread biscuits all over the pan and bake for 12 minutes till biscuits become lightly browned. Remove from oven and sprinkle fresh parsley on it. Serve and enjoy

Cast Iron Tomato-Feta Strata

Ingredients
- 1/2 cup of low-fat yogurt
- 4 large eggs
- 3 tbsp. Parsley, sliced
- 1 medium onion, thinly sliced
- 1 tbsp olive oil
- 1 large thinly chopped garlic clove
- One 16-ounce can diced tomatoes with their juices
- 1/2 teaspoon crushed red pepper
- 5 ounces whole wheat peasant bread, cut into 1-inch cubes (4 cups)
- Salt and freshly ground pepper
- 2 ounces feta cheese, crumble

Method

- Preheat oven to 450°.
- Whisk eggs, yogurt and parsley together in a medium bowl.
- Heat the oil in a 10-inch skillet and add garlic, onion, crushed red pepper and sage. Sauté over high heat and stir often till the onion becomes slightly browned and softened, about three minutes. Stir in the tomatoes with its juice. Season with pepper and salt and allow simmering. Add the bread and sprinkle with feta cheese. Ladle on egg mixture, baking for 20 mins, till turned golden brown. Leave to cool slightly and enjoy.

Cast Iron Spanish Baked Eggs With Chorizo

Ingredients:

- 4 eggs
- 1 onion, diced
- 2 gloves of garlic, crushed
- 1 medium chorizo sausage, sliced
- 1 cup of tinned tomatoes
- 1 tbsp mixed herbs
- Crusty bread, to serve

Method:

- Heat a splash of olive oil in your skillet on a medium heat. Add the garlic, onion and chorizo and fry for 3 minutes. Add the tomatoes and mixed herbs and simmer for 5 minutes.
- With a large spoon, make 4 pools in the sauce and crack the eggs into these dips. Cover with a lid and cook for 10 minutes.
- Serve with fresh, crusty bread and enjoy!

One Pan English breakfast

Ingredients:

- 4 eggs, whisked
- 2 low fat sausages, sliced
- 4 rashers of back bacon, cut into strips
- 2 medium tomatoes, sliced
- 6 medium mushrooms, sliced
- 1 tin baked beans, to serve

Method:

- In a heated skillet, place the sausage and bacon and fry for 4 minutes, stirring occasionally. Add the mushrooms and cook for a further 4 minutes.
- Add the tomatoes and season the mixture with salt and pepper. Reduce to a low heat and pour over the whisked eggs, covering and cooking for a 5 minutes, until the eggs are cooked.
- Leave to cool for 5 minutes to allow the eggs to set. Serve with baked beans and crusty bread for a beautiful breakfast or brunch.

Cast Iron Deluxe Smoked Salmon and Chive Scrambled Eggs

Ingredients:

- 4 eggs, whisked
- 200g smoked salmon, sliced
- A bunch of chives, chopped
- 1 tbsp crème fraiche
- Wholegrain toast, to serve

Method:

- Heat a knob of butter in the skillet over a low heat. Mix the crème fraiche with the whisked eggs, season, then pour into the skillet.
- Stir every minute, until the eggs begin to solidify. After around 5 minutes, while the eggs are still partially liquefied, add the smoked salmon and chives. Cook for a further 2 minutes.
- Serve on buttered, wholegrain toast and enjoy!

Cast Iron Perfect Peanut Butter Pancakes with Blueberries

Ingredients:

- 130g plain flour
- 1 tsp baking powder
- 2 tbsp caster sugar
- 130 ml milk
- 1 egg, whisked
- 2 tbsp peanut butter
- 2 cups of blueberries, to serve

Method:

- Sift the flour, baking powder and sugar into a bowl. In a separate bowl, whisk together the egg, milk and peanut butter.
- Combine the two mixtures and stir thoroughly until not lumps remain in the batter.
- Heat a knob of butter in your skillet. Spoon a ladle of batter onto the pan and cook until the top of the pancake begins to bubble. Flip the pancake and cook until the underside is golden brown.
- Repeat with the remaining batter. Serve in a heaped pile, sprinkling over blueberries and drizzling over honey if desired. Delicious!

Cast Iron Spiced Stewed Fruit with Crunchy Granola Yoghurt

Ingredients:

- 2 cups blueberries
- 2 cups chopped apple
- 1 tbsp cinnamon
- ½ cup of caster sugar
- 1 cup of water
- 2 cups of low fat Greek yoghurt
- 2 cups of granola

Method:

- Melt a knob of butter in a heated skillet over a medium heat. Add the fruit and sprinkle over the cup of sugar and cinnamon.
- Pour over the water and cover, simmering for 10 minutes and stirring occasionally. Remove the lid and allow cooling for 20 minutes.
- In separate bowls, place the yoghurt and sprinkle over the granola evenly. Spoon over the deliciously thick stewed fruit and enjoy a simple and healthy breakfast.

Cast Iron Bacon and Spinach Potato Cakes with Fried Egg

Ingredients:

- 4 rashers of smoked back bacon, sliced
- 4 cups of spinach
- 3 large white potatoes, quartered and peeled
- 4 eggs
- 1 cup mature cheddar, grated
- 1 bowl of plain flour, sifted

Method:

- In a large saucepan, bring water to the boil. Place the potatoes into the water and cook for 10 minutes, or until soft. Drain and return to the pan and mash, adding butter and salt to taste. Put aside and cook for at least 20 minutes.
- Place your skillet pan on a medium heat and fry the bacon for 3-4 minutes, until the fat is golden brown. Place the spinach on the pan and wilt for 2 minutes. Allow to cool for 5 minutes.
- Combine the spinach and bacon with the potato mixture and stir, sprinkling in the cheese gradually. Shape the mixture into rounded patties, rolling in the flour for extra crispiness.
- Heat 2 tbsp of oil in the skillet and fry the potato cakes for 5 minutes on each side, until crispy and golden brown. Fry the eggs and place on top of the cakes for a hearty breakfast.

Cast Iron Roasted Red Pepper and Feta Cheese Omelet

Ingredients:

- 2 red bell peppers
- 1 cup of crumbled feta cheese
- 6 eggs, whisked

Method:

- Place the peppers whole into an oven preheated to 180C. Roast in the oven for 20 minutes, until the skin has partially blackened. Allow to cool, peel of the blackened skin then slice the peppers into medium strips.
- Heat a splash of olive oil in the skillet and add the peppers. Pour over the whisked eggs and season. Cook for 5 minutes until the top is bubbling then sprinkle over the feta cheese.
- Flip the omelet and cook the underside for a further 2 minutes. Serve with rocket salad or buttered toast.

Cast Iron Fabulous French Toast with Maple Syrup and Pecans

Ingredients:

- 4 eggs
- 4 slices of 2-3 day old bread
- 1 cup milk
- 1cup maple syrup
- 1 cup pecan nuts

Method:

- Mix together the eggs and milk. Place the bread into the bowl and allow the bread to absorb the mixture for 1-2 minutes. Repeat for the remainder of the bread.
- Heat a knob of butter in the skillet over a medium flame. Place the bread, two at a time, into the pan and cook for 1-2 minutes on each side until the bread is golden brown and crispy.
- After serving, sprinkle over the pecans evenly and drizzle over the maple syrup for a beautiful breakfast!

Cast Iron Asparagus and Parmesan Potato Pancakes

Ingredients:

- 10 asparagus spears

- 1 cup parmesan
- 2 medium white potatoes, peeled and sliced
- 4 eggs

Method:

- Heat a knob of butter over a medium flame in your skillet. Cook the potato slices for 3 minutes on each side. Add the asparagus and cook for 2 minutes.
- Meanwhile, mix the eggs and parmesan in a bowl and pour over the vegetables in the pan. Cover and cook for a further 5 minutes. Once cooked through, slice into squares and serve for a deliciously healthy breakfast!

Cast Iron Skillet Pizza Breakfast

Ingredients

- Bread dough or Homemade Pizza
- Pizza sauce
- Olive Oil

- Any desired cooked Breakfast toppings (Hash browns ,Left over Home fries, diced ham , crumbled bacon, , etc)
- 1 raw egg per mini Pizza
- Shredded mozzarella
- Salt and Pepper to taste

Method

- Flatten the dough in warm greased cast iron skillet. Brush oil on the flattened dough and add toppings and sauce. Set aside in warm place in order to allow dough raise for fifteen to thirteen minutes. Mould the mozzarella into a nest and slip the raw egg in the nest. Add pepper and salt as preferred.

- Preheat your oven to 375°. Once raised, bake 12-20 minutes or until the egg becomes opaque on top. If bottom starts to turn brown before top gets done, turn over on broiler to also cook the top. Watch them closely.

- Mix half BBQ sauce with half pizza sauce together. Use shredded or little chunks of thoroughly cooked chicken, Mozzarella cheese, chopped fresh basil leaves, egg, pepper and salt. Or as preferred

Cast Iron Roasted Brussels Sprouts Recipe

Ingredients
- 1 tablespoon minced garlic (about 3 cloves)
- 1 pound Brussels sprouts, rinsed, end trimmed, rough outer leaves of larger sprouts removed
- 2 Tbsp olive oil
- 1 teaspoon lemon juice
- Freshly ground black pepper
- 1/4 cup freshly grated Parmesan cheese (optional)
- Salt

Method

- Pre-heat your oven to 350°F. Set brussels sprouts in a skillet. Add in garlic and sprinkle lemon juice on the brussels sprouts. Add olive oil in order to ensure sprouts are coated thoroughly. Add little turns of black pepper and at least, sprinkle half teaspoon of salt.

- Ladle the brussels sprouts on top rack in the oven and cook for twenty minutes. Stir to ensure sprouts are well coated with olive oil and also cook for an additional ten minutes. As desired, sprinkle in Parmesan, and Cook for another five minutes.
- *Hint: timing should be based on the size of sprouts and your oven, in particular. Sprouts should be browned with some of its exterior leaves crunchy and its interior cooked through. Should in case sprouts look like they appear too browned, then lower the heat or move them to a lower rack.*
- Salt should be added to taste as its key to getting the best out of this recipe.

Andouille Sausage Skillet Pasta

Ingredients
- 2 cups chicken broth
- 2 cloves of garlic(minced)
- 1 tablespoon olive oil
- 1(12.8-ounce)thinly sliced of packaged smoked andouille sausage
- ½ cup milk
- 8 ounces elbows pasta
- 1 can(14.5-ounce) of diced tomatoes
- 1 onion(diced)
- 1 cup shredded pepper jack cheese

- Kosher salt and freshly ground black pepper, to taste

Method

In a large cast iron skillet, heat oil, over med. high heat. Adding onion, sausage and garlic, cook and stir often, till sausage becomes browned (lightly), about three to four minutes.

Ladle in tomatoes, pasta, chicken broth and milk. Seasoning with pepper and salt to taste, leave to boil and cover it up. Lower the heat and leave to simmer till the pasta is thoroughly cooked, about twelve to fourteen mins.

Remove from the heat and add cheese on top .then cover till cheese has thoroughly melted, for two minutes and serve at once. Enjoy your breakfast.

Italian Chicken, Mushroom, And Zucchini Skillet

Ingredients

- 2 squares Italian Herb Sauté Express® Sauté Starter
- 1 pound chicken breasts (cut in half) or tenderloins
- ½ yellow onion, diced
- 2 teaspoons olive oil
- 12 ounces mushrooms, sliced
- 3 cloves garlic, minced
- 2/3 cup sundried tomatoes
- 2 zucchini, cut in bite-size chunks
- 1 teaspoon Italian seasoning

- 2 15-ounce cans fire roasted diced tomatoes
- 1 teaspoon balsamic vinegar (optional)
- Salt and pepper, to taste

Method

- Melt the Sauté Express® Sauté Starter over medium heat in large cast iron skillet. Heat till it starts to bubble and pat dry chicken on each side. Toss in chicken and sauté till browned or for five to seven minutes. Turn the other side of chicken and cook the till well browned. Meanwhile, brush some Sauté Express® Sauté Starter on the chicken side that is facing up.

- Remove the chicken from and place aside in a plate. Pour oil into your skillet and set it over medium heat. Cook the onion for three minutes. Toss in mushrooms and keep on cooking for five mins. Add the sundried tomatoes, zucchini and garlic. Cook for two minutes. Add the Italian seasoning, diced tomatoes, pepper and salt. If desired, ladle in balsamic vinegar.

- Place chicken back in the cast iron skillet and scoop some of the veggies and sauce over the chicken. Covered and cook in the oven at 350°F or over the stovetop till chicken is thoroughly cooked and the sauce starts to bubble.

Cinnamon Crunch Skillet Bread

Ingredients

Preparing the dough:

- 3 Tbsp. white sugar
- 1 1/2 tsp. fine salt
- 3 cups all purpose flour
- 1 cup milk, warmed to 105-110° F.
- 3 Tbsp. vegetable oil or melted butter
- 3 tsp. instant or dry active yeast

Dough brushing :

- 1/2 tsp. Vanilla
- 1/3 cup butter, melted

For coating the dough in:

- 3/4 cup brown sugar
- 1 1/2 tsp. cinnamon
- Streusel topping:
- 1/4 cup brown sugar
- 1 tablespoon butter, cold
- 1 teaspoon cinnamon
- Glaze:
- 2 cups icing/confectioners' sugar
- 2 Tbsp. maple syrup
- 1/4 cup milk
- 1/4 cup butter, melted
- 1 tsp. vanilla
- 1/8 teaspoon Salt

Method

- Make the dough: Proof the yeast in 1/4 cup of warm water. Combine the dry ingredients in a large bowl or the bowl of a stand mixer. Add the warmed milk, vegetable oil and proofed yeast. Knead with the dough hook until dough is smooth, adding more flour by the Tbsp. as necessary. Remove dough to an oiled bowl, cover with plastic wrap and let rise to doubled, about 60 minutes.
- Grease a skillet and set aside.
- Divide dough into two pieces and roll into a rope about 3 feet long. Place the dough on to a long piece or parchment or foil wrap and liberally brush with melted butter mixed with the

vanilla. Then pour the mixture of cinnamon/sugar,evenly with buttered ropes and roll the them thoroughly in the mixture till evenly covered and pinch the rope ends together and twist. pinch second end once and twist all together.

- Place twisted ropes into the skillet, starting from the centre and winding it around. (If you have some melted butter left over from brushing, feel free to drizzle it over the dough). Cover the skillet with greased plastic wrap and let rise until doubled.
- Meanwhile, prepare the streusel topping by combining dry ingredients and cutting in the cold butter with a fork. Set aside.
- Preheat oven to 350° F. Once dough is doubled, sprinkle with streusel topping and bake for 40-45 minutes, covering it with foil after 25 or 30 minutes if is dark enough.
- Meanwhile, prepare the glaze by combining the wet ingredients and adding to the powdered sugar. Stir well until smooth. Pour evenly over bread once it has cooled a bit.

Polenta Skillet Eggs with Chorizo

Ingredients:

- ¾ Cup dry polenta or corn meal
- 1 Cup of grated melting cheese (cheddar ,jack, mozzarella)
- 8 oz chorizo (links or ground) browned
- ½ teaspoon of paprika(smoked)
- ¼ cilantro (chopped and divided)
- ½ chicken stock
- 6 eggs
- Pepper and salt to taste

Method

- Pre-heat your oven to 400°F.Brown chorizo or sausage using a cast iron skillet and place aside. Add the stock and bring it to a boil, using the same skillet. Reduce heat to medium low and toss in smoked paprika and polenta. Whisk vigorously in order to avoid clumping. Once thoroughly whisked, cover and lower the heat to cook for fifteen minutes. Stir occasionally, add in the grated cheese and stir to mix thoroughly. Fold in half of the chorizo (or sausage), half of the diced cilantro. If necessary, add salt to taste (because if you are using chorizo and chicken stock, they are naturally salty).Make your polenta flavourful and add pepper to taste.

- Set, in the centre, the second half of chorizo on top of polenta. Using a spoon, make small indentations (circles) within the polenta for the eggs to rest, just around outer edges of your cast iron skillet. Break the eggs and set them in the indentations. Add pepper and salt lightly on each egg. Set the skillet in the preheated oven, baking till egg whites and yolks become white and set. Cook till you reached your desired doneness). I often broil for just one minute. Then garnish with the remaining cilantro and hot sauce Hint: You could add a bed sautéed peppers, sautéed spinach, sautéed mushrooms and sautéed onions to it and by placing polenta on top, right beneath the eggs.

Cast Iron Skillet Potato Cake

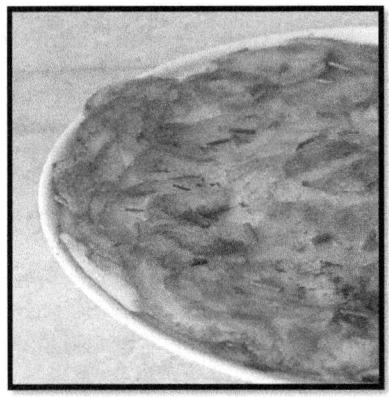

Ingredients

- 6 potatoes peeled

- 1/2 stick unsalted butter

- 1/2 teaspoon black pepper

- 2 teaspoons chopped rosemary
  Chives for garnish

- 1 teaspoon kosher salt

Method

- Melt butter and simmer gently, in a cast iron skillet. Slowly pour butter into a bowl when milk solids begin to sink to bottom. Keep as much of white milky liquid as you in the skillet and pour away the milk solids placed aside.

- Slice all the potatoes to thin (1/8inch) slices. I make use of my trusty mandolin to make sure they become as thin as possible.

- Ladle them onto a bowl, covering with 3/4 of melted butter. Then season with little rosemary, pepper and salt. Toss in order to coat potatoes with the melted butter. Spoon remaining butter within the bottom of the skillet and swirl around to thoroughly coat the sides and bottom.

- Set the potatoes in layer and press them down gently to ensure they start sticking together to form a cake. Set your cast iron skillet on stove top applying medium high heat; cook till edges begins to turn brown, for five to eight minutes. Then place skillet in oven, heated at about 400°F.Cook till potatoes start to feel tender within the centre when pressed with a fork. Lower the temp. to about 350°F if the potatoes begin to brown very fast

- Remove skillet and carefully discard excess liquid or butter that might have formed on the bottom. Set skillet on flat surface, covering with a platter slightly larger than the skillet. Turn platter over but rather carefully. Lifting off skillet, use large spatula to transfer it back into the skillet. Ladle the butter back in and sauté in the oven for an extra five to eight minutes and remove from oven. Discard any liquid, garnishing with chives and then serve.

Skillet Steaks with Gorgonzola Herbed Butter

Ingredients
Preparing the steaks:

- salt and fresh ground pepper
- olive oil
- 4 ribeye steaks, or your preferred cut

Herbed butter:

- 1 tbsp. fresh parsley, chopped
- 4 tbsp. Gorgonzola cheese
- 4 tbsp. butter, softened

Method

- Season all sides of the steaks with fresh ground pepper and salt. Then tightly wrap each steak in a plastic wrap. Set them in your refrigerator, overnight or for few hrs. Remove them from refrigerator, for thirty minutes before cooking so as to ensure the steaks reach room temperature.
- Heat a large skillet over med. Heat (you could use an open flame with grate if camping or a side burner on a grill).
- Sprinkle oil onto bottom of the cast iron skillet and ensure its well-coated. Place each steak into the skillet and cook over the medium heat for two minutes. Flip and sauté the second side of the steak for 2 minutes or cook longer for desired level of doneness. Remove from heat, leave to cool for 5 minutes in the cast iron skillet.

Herbed butter:

- Cream Gorgonzola cheese, fresh parsley and butter together and place 1 tbsp herbed butter onto top of each steak and leave to melt over each side as serving.

www.ingramcontent.com/pod-product-compliance
Lightning Source LLC
Chambersburg PA
CBHW060348290526
45791CB00004B/1580